ENCAMPED

─✿✿ ABOUT WITH ✿✿─

FEAR

Carolyn Granderson

WESTBOW
PRESS®
A DIVISION OF THOMAS NELSON
& ZONDERVAN

This book is a work of non-fiction. Unless otherwise noted, the author and the publisher make no explicit guarantees as to the accuracy of the information contained in this book and in some cases, names of people and places have been altered to protect their privacy.

WestBow Press books may be ordered through booksellers or by contacting:

WestBow Press
A Division of Thomas Nelson & Zondervan
1663 Liberty Drive
Bloomington, IN 47403
www.westbowpress.com
1 (866) 928-1240

Scripture taken from the King James Version of the Bible.

ISBN: 978-1-9736-9227-0 (sc)
ISBN: 978-1-9736-9226-3 (hc)
ISBN: 978-1-9736-9228-7 (e)

Library of Congress Control Number: 2020909140

Print information available on the last page.

WestBow Press rev. date: 06/26/2020

CONTENTS

INTRODUCTION

I was raised in a small town in the Sierra Mountains. The gigantic evergreen trees would appear at night as monsters. My childhood memories of being afraid were those of the haunted house, scary movies, and being outside after dark. I would go to my friend's house during the day and play until the sun started to go down. The pathway home was surrounded by these monstrous trees. I would sprint home because of my imaginary fears.

But, there were also real things to fear in the mountains; deer, large tarantula spiders, rattle snakes, bears and mountain lions made their homes in the areas surrounding our community. I was afraid to venture far away from home. Living in the heart of the mountains as a young child was fun, full of excitement, and at times, very scary.

My childhood fears seemed to vanish as I grew older. I would go out alone late at night and never think about what might happen. There were times when I would find myself in life-threatening situations and was able to calmly get out of them. I lived in a dangerous environment and sometimes was faced with situations that could be a cause for alarm. Fear seemed to no longer be an issue.

After becoming a mother, nerve racking situations seem to be just a way of life: my six year old son, running inside crying, with a huge purple bump on his forehead because he had fallen off his bike; my four year old daughter falling into a glass window and cutting her forehead open; my young teenage son going to a basketball game, not letting me know where he was going after the game, and I am frantically searching for him. My thoughts were *this is just a part of parenting.*

I began to notice, after my children became teenagers, my uneasy feelings turned into fears. One day my children decided they wanted to go to a church event out of town and my oldest son was driving. I felt they would be home by twelve a.m. It was difficult for me to sleep. I kept listening for the door to open. It was after one o'clock. Unable to stay in bed my first impulse was to walk and pray. My mind started to image them in a horrible automobile accident and tears ran down my face. I could no longer take the feelings I was experiencing. I called my neighbor sobbing and told her my children were not home. Crying I asked her to *pray.* Minutes later my children entered the house, saw me crying, and asked "Mom, what's wrong?" All I could do was cry. My fears seemed to increase as my children became more independent.

My everyday life was being affected by fear. I stopped listening to the news. I was afraid one of my children might be involved in a terrible crime or horrible accident. Situations would happen and cause me to think, *I handled that situation incorrectly.* The nervousness about my choices would turn on the tears and I would begin to struggle within myself, only to find out that everything was alright. Fear was putting pressure on my life

To add to the pressures already existing, I was involved in an automobile accident. My car was hit on the front passenger side. It was turned around headed back into the oncoming traffic. After the car stopped, I sat shocked. I saw smoke coming from the engine compartment. I opened the door to try to get out, but couldn't, my clothes were caught on something. I ripped my dress from whatever was holding it and ran back across the street. I remember hearing people telling me not to run. Thankfully, God blessed me not to get hit by the traffic and there were no injuries. But, I began to cry hysterically after I saw the cars that were involved in the accident and the people around me. I felt it was my fault.

Several months later I went to the mailbox and

found a letter from a lawyer stating that I was going to be sued for one hundred thousand dollars. As I read the letter my stomach tightened, my heart beat rapidly, my breathing changed and once again tears flowed. Several weeks later I received another letter from the lawyer and also from my insurance company. My insurance lawyer wanted me to come into his office. He wanted to question me about the accident. I noticed that whenever the mail drop into the mailbox I would become nervous and my mind started to play back the accident. People would tell me, "They can only get what the insurance allows." But, fear was still there. My mind was full of doubt. I tried to talk about what I was feeling, but people didn't seem to understand. They would say "you're a *Christian* you shouldn't worry." The thought of being sued was overwhelming.

I had been a Christian for many years. I was faithful in church and believed the bible was the true word of God. I prayed for people believing for healing and deliverance. I would periodically preach the word of God to the congregation where I attended church. Something was happening now that I was trying to understand. What was happening to me was not pleasant. As a spirit filled believer I knew God was always present with me, but I found myself encamped about with fear, never realizing fear was imprisonment.

Fear was trying to find a place to lodge in my mind where it could control my behavior. The word of God says *fear is torment*. However, I was unaware of what that really meant.

ENCAMPED ABOUT WITH FEAR

I had been experiencing certain feelings. At home when I would hear the mailman drop the mail into the box, my stomach would become jittery. I began to think someone was sending bad news. I would hear the news reports about an accident and wonder if it involved one of my children. At work something would happen. My heart would begin to pound in my chest, and I would begin to wonder, *What will happen because of this situation?* These situations would leave me breathless and weak.

I did not know what was happening. But one day while on the way to the store, listening to the radio, I heard an advertisement. It gave me the definition of anxiety. If you are experiencing palpitations, sweating, shortness of breath, jittery stomach, and feeling of imminent disaster (something about to happen that could be disastrous) that lasts from a few second to an hour or more, you may be experiencing anxiety attacks. Immediately I realized this is what I had been experiencing. I rushed to tell my daughter, excited to know what was happening to me. When I told her, she gasped and said, "Oh, mom, no." I realized at that moment what was happening was not good. These anxiety attacks had been increasing within the last two years. I had to know more.

I began to research anxiety attacks. One of the things I discovered was that they are stress related. The author of *Anxiety and Panic Attacks* talked about how your mind is creating a "haunted house" that is not there. When I was young, I went to the fair with my friends. They wanted to ride through the haunted house. As we rode through, I never saw what was before me because I had my eyes closed and only screamed when I heard my friends scream. I was afraid to look. I wanted to jump out and run, but I just held on. Was this what I had been doing for years? Was I not noticing what was happening to me? I was unaware that if I allowed a thought or a feeling of fear to be left to the imagination, it could quickly get out of hand and grow into something that was terrifying. This is why we have to face the truth no matter what it is; we cannot leave the unknown in our mind.

After researching, I found that relaxing the body

and the mind are important in helping to release stress. Exercise and rest are what the body needs to relax. What about the mind? The word of God came to my memory.

> Finally, brethren, whatsoever things are true, whatsoever things are honest, whatsoever things are just, whatsoever things are pure, whatsoever things are of good report; if there be any virtue, and if there be any praise, think on these things. (Philippians 4:8)

I remember coming home from work. I would cook and prepare my husband's lunch, see him off to work, clean up, and lie down to rest. My mind would start to think about what had happened during the day, and the negative thoughts would come. I started second-guessing what I had done during the day. After a time of fretting and contemplating, I realized my adversary, fear, was attacking my judgment. I began to apply the word of God to my life. I began to think of Philippians 4:8. I began to think about the good times I had had as a child with my dad. I listened to the audio Bible and read books that would encourage me. I thought about the wonderful things God has in store for those who believe. Emerging ourselves into the things of God is an effective tool to fight off negative thoughts that come to our mind.

Relaxing the mind helps to focus on the positive. In Joel 3, God tells the people to prepare for war, and as they prepared, he tells them in verse 10 of chapter 3, "Beat your plowshares into swords and your pruning hooks into spears: let the weak say, I am strong." There was a war that was going on in my mind, and I had to be positive. I found it helpful to make a list of positive attributes about myself. This was reassuring when I began to feel down and ineffective. When I found myself concentrating on negative thoughts, I reminded myself that God loved me and that "I can do all things through Christ which strengtheneth me" (Philippians 4:13). That assurance gave rest to my mind.

I realized the importance of having a positive outlook. Hebrews 11:1 says, "Now faith is the substance of things hoped for, the evidence of things not seen." I believe having faith brings about better health, behavior changes, and any improvement you want to make. The Bible says in Hebrews 11:6, "But, without faith it is impossible to please him: For he that cometh to God must believe that he is and that he is a rewarder of them that diligently seek him." Having the faith to believe that God can do whatever we need him to do will result in having everything we need and those things that we want. Through prayer I was able to get into a place in my mind where I could talk to God. It was a secret place, a resting place, and a place where I can think positive thoughts.

Having control of your mind is the beginning of deliverance. When negative and/or irrational thoughts come to your mind, reject them. One young lady said she had to force them out of her mind. Just refuse to think on them. The enemy used these thoughts to try to lower my self-esteem and impact my life. Satan is a liar, an accuser of the brethren; he uses his craftiness to bring fear into our minds. He provides mental pictures and emotional feelings that try to tear down our image of ourselves and create a feeling of fear because of our choices. Feelings of being inferior can arise, but when the spirit of Christ lives within us, we are superior, righteous, and holy! We must know that God has created us and that we are his children. Daily reminders of who we are help the mind to make the body feel complete in Christ.

The word of God tells us, "Where there is no vision the people parish" (Proverbs 29:18). Vision, as described in a Bible reference, is "a sight (mentally), dream, revelation, or oracle" *(Strong's Exhaustive Concordance of the Bible)*. The New King James Version says, "Where there is no revelation, the people cast off restraint." The word *restraint* means control of emotions, impulses, etc. *(Webster's New World*

Dictionary). What God had revealed to me was to take control of my thoughts. God wanted me to stop visualizing the negative and focus on the positive promises of God and to control my emotions. Stop crying! Second Corinthians 10:5 says, "Casting down imaginations and every high thing that exalteth itself against the knowledge of God, and bringing into captivity every thought to the obedience of Christ." God wanted me to reflect on the things that are pleasing in his sight and to submit to his control. I was visualizing things that had not taken place, and these thoughts would cause spiritual destruction. Our insight must be biblical.

Satan will always try to talk to your mind, but when he is talking, refuse to listen. Replace negative and irrational thoughts with reality. We have to be mindful of what is real and the tricks of the enemy. Philippians 2:5 states, "Let this mind be in you, which was also in Christ Jesus." A renewing of my mind was necessary. The enemy is out to destroy our minds. The devil tried to talk to Jesus and tried to cause him to lose his focus. He tried to distort the Savior's vision when he was on the mountain. But because of the love Christ had for humankind, he rebuked the devil and continued on to the cross. As a human, the Lord was despised and rejected, but he never lost focus of his purpose, and I could not lose mine.

In researching, it became clearer to me about the mind and negative thoughts being the start of all my feeling. Could it be that stress brought about anxiety, anxiety brought about an anxiety attack, and the anxiety attack brought about panic and phobia that cause illness, both mentally and physically? Could they all be components of fear?

I searched Rothenberg and Chapman's medical dictionary to see what was said regarding anxiety, anxiety attacks, panic, and phobia.

- anxiety: state of mild to severe apprehension often without specific cause
- anxiety attacks: acute episodes of intense anxiety and feelings of panic
- panic: intense, overwhelming *fear* producing terror, physiological changes, and often immobility or hysterical behavior
- phobia: anxiety disorder characterized by irrational and intense *fear* of an object and activity or physical conditions; the intense *fear* usually causes tremor, panic, palpitations, nausea, and other physical signs

I had named the spirit that had been surrounding me *fear*. Now what do you do? You take action. This spirit was powerful and controlling. Elijah, a man of

God, bold, ruthless toward evil, righteous, who spoke the word of God, after he had challenged the prophets of Bail and God answered his prayers, went into hiding because of the fear of Jezebel. She had "bewitched him" concerning his life. Along with the spirit of fear comes the spirit of discouragement. Elijah became discouraged and sat under a juniper tree. Fearful that he was the only one left who trusted God, he fled. I could identify with Elijah. I felt I was alone. I couldn't tell anyone the impact this attack had upon my life. I am a Christian. I felt I had to handle this alone. But I realized I was not alone. Christ was with me. I knew this spirit of fear had to be destroyed. The word of God became my defense.

Second Corinthians 10:4 says, "For the weapons of our warfare are not carnal, but mighty through God to the pulling down of strongholds." Where were the strongholds? They were in my mind. I could not nurse this spirit or show it sympathy; it had to die. I read a statement from *Word Aflame,* a Sunday school book, that stated, "Thoughts have their own self-life and no thought or idea graciously accepts death." This is why the Word must be written on the tables of our heart— so we can have a word for the enemy. The thoughts that were coming to my mind must become captive to the obedience of Christ. I knew there would be a struggle because we have to fight against our very own nature; we have to bring our mind and flesh into the obedience of God's word.

Realizing this is a spiritual battle, I knew prayer was necessary. My communication with Christ was what was going to help me to be victorious. Through asking God and waiting for his answer, I would become more like Christ and bring my thoughts into subjection. I had to take authority over the spirit of fear. The writer also stated that as well as thoughts having their own self-life, "they are sustained by our willingness to accept them." Christ spoke to the spirits that had the mind of the man in Mark 1:25. Jesus rebuked them. "Hold thy peace and come out of him." I had to take that same authority and have faith.

Where there is fear, there is no faith (Mark 4:40). What did this mean? What is fear? *Webster's* definition says, "Fear is a feeling of anxiety caused by the presence or nearness of danger, evil, pain etc." What is faith? *Webster* describes it as "unquestioning belief that does not require proof or evidence." I was telling myself the situations in my life were going to cause disastrous results. But I had to remind myself that God has his plan for my life and all things, whether pleasing or uncomfortable, work for my growth. I had to believe this without proof or evidence. God's will is good for my life now and for the future. God allows things we don't totally understand, but whatever he allows is part of his master plan. God will not cause me to be in a position that I cannot go through successfully. His will for my life is complete in all respects. It is excellent. His word lets me know that my life will be victorious if I keep the mind of Christ and keep the faith. We must rely on God with the assurance that anything that we need, God is going to supply, even though we don't see it.

Faith is empowerment. The word says if we have the faith of a grain of a mustard seed, we can speak to the mountain to be removed and it will be done. Faith gives us authority. I had to act upon my faith by listening to what God was saying to me through his word. I had to understand my feelings; I had to know that I could overcome any obstacle; I had to listen to wise counsel; I had to describe the positive and create positive thoughts. I had to create a turnaround in my thinking and replace fear with faith!

Our God is powerful and able to defeat any demonic spirit. Mark 5 tells of a man with an unclean spirit. (Foul, offensive, impure, filthy, hateful, disgraceful, loud, low-self-esteem, and fearful definition from *Webster's New World Dictionary*). People saw him as being mad. They tried to capture him and bind him, but he was too strong to hold. He must have felt the pain of his sufferings and cried out night and day. He cut his flesh with stones. One day Jesus came by, and when he saw Jesus, he ran and worshipped him. In verse 7, the man asked Jesus not to torment him. Jesus, knowing this man was being tormented, asked, "What is your name?" He answered, "Legion, for we are many." The demons begged Jesus not to send them out into the country. Jesus told them to come out and sent them into a herd of swine. The swine ran down from the mountain into the water, and they drowned. After the people of the city heard the good thing Jesus had done, they were afraid. I found it strange for the people to be fearful after a great miracle was done. I wondered if some place in the people's minds, they had told themselves that this good thing was bad. Fear causes you to refuse to see the positive in a situation. The Bible tells me all things work together for good to them who are called according to his—God's— purpose. I realized that God was going to make a way of escape if I would use my authority.

God had shown his wonderful works in my life, but the unclean spirits that are in the world today had begun to torment my mind; there seemed to be many. Someone would say something, and my mind started to pick up feelings of hurt, discouragement, and doubt and then become offensive and critical. I realized this thing was getting bigger than I wanted it to become in my life, and it caused me to cry out. I fasted and prayed, but there seem to be no relief, no complete deliverance. I had to seek after a deeper relationship with Jesus. He had never failed before, and I knew he was the same God now.

The man with the unclean spirits ran and worshiped Jesus. In this scripture, worship means he kissed him like a dog licks the hand of his master *(Strong's Concordance)*. Jesus knew the kind of spirits this man had. Jesus knows the heart, motive, and thoughts of man. After these spirits had been removed, the man sat clothed and in his right mind. I wanted to say like David in Psalm 51:10, "Create in me a clean heart, O God and renew a right spirit within me." I wanted to be in my right mind (a rational mind), thinking rationally.

The spirit of the Lord let me know that this spirit of fear was not just one spirit but many with others that come under the category of fear. It is like a potato when it is put in water. The buds or eyes develop into new stems that product different sizes and shapes of potatoes. A friend referred to fear as an umbrella term for the evil it covers. The psalmist David said in Psalm 56:2, "Mine enemies would daily swallow me up: for they fight against me, O thou most high." He continues in Psalm 56:3. "What time I am afraid I will trust in thee." It was time for me to put my trust totally in the Lord for my deliverance. Because fear has so many ways to manifest itself into our lives, I had to realize that this is a constant battle.

GOD'S WORD COMBATS THE ENEMY

Anything that is not of God is an enemy of God. Mark 5:35–41 says that while Jesus was talking, there came from the ruler of the synagogue's house people who said that the master's daughter had died. Jesus heard the word that was spoken. He told the ruler of the synagogue not to be afraid but only believe. He came into the house of the ruler of the synagogue and saw the house in an uproar with people crying loudly. When he came in, he asked them why they were crying, the damsel is not dead, but is sleeping. The people laughed. He put them all out and took the father and the mother and entered in where the damsel was lying. He took the damsel by the hand and said, "Talotha cumi," which is interpreted, "Damsel, I say unto thee, arise: and she arose and walked."

It appeared to the people she was dead, and when Jesus said she was asleep, they laughed. Jesus dismissed all those who did not believe. He took her parents, those that were willing to believe, and spoke to the girl. She arose and walked. The Lord was looking for those with faith to believe he was able to do what seems impossible. God's word will combat the enemy if we only have faith and believe. He will dismiss the doubt and take our hand to bring us through.

Fears are real, and when some people hear your fears, they may laugh and say, "That is crazy." But these feelings do exist. You try to explain what you feel to others, and when they do not understand, you find yourself feeling that you are alone. I felt I could not tell anyone the fears I had because of the thoughts they might have about me. One young lady stated it this way: "Fear wants to back you into a corner and make you feel that you are alone." Jesus realized that we would have these feeling of being alone, and he said that he would never leave us alone.

As I continued to focus on God's word to receive insight, I read 1 John 4:18. It said, "There is no fear in love; but perfect love casteth out fear: because fear hath torment. He that feareth is not made perfect in love." Did I not truly love God? I was so bounded and tormented by fear that I was losing sight on love. It was time to refocus. It was difficult because I didn't really understand "love." But I knew I had to let go of fear when I read that the fearful and unbelieving will find themselves in the lake that burns with fire and brimstone (Rev. 21:8).

I knew I was not going to let fear take me to that place. I had to search for a deeper relationship with my God. God offers his love freely, but we have to search the word and apply it to our lives. It is more than reading the word, hiding the word in our heart, or speaking the word; it is an understanding of how to apply the word to our lives. It's getting close enough to the word that it speaks to you. I had to surrender over to God my body, mind, and soul. I had to choose who I was going to love with all my heart and faithfully serve.

IS YOUR MIND A TRASH CAN FOR THE DEVIL?

I was allowing the spirit of fear to use my mind as a trash can. When my mind was being used as a trash can, it was being bombarded with lies, threats, accusations, death threats, fear of man, terrors, horror stories, and doubt. The mind was where the battle was being fought. Jesus had to fight battles, and he always had a spiritual answer for the devil and those who doubted. Jesus was tempted in the wilderness by the devil and his spiritual weapon was the word; "It is written" and "Get thee hence (depart)." I had to combat the enemy of my mind with the word of God.

I read in Judges about the children of Israel who did evil in the sight of the Lord. They allowed their minds to be influence by the thinking of their enemy. The things they knew to be true were now becoming tainted by the lifestyle of the enemy. They had been mightily oppressed for twenty years, but the Lord heard their cry and rose up Deborah, a prophetess, wife, and judge of Israel. She sent for Barak and asked him did not the Lord tell him to go and take 10,000 men to the river of Kishon and he will deliver the enemy into his hands? Barak acknowledged what the Lord had said, and he said he would go if Deborah would go with him. She agreed to go with him.

Sisera, the captain of the army, heard that Barak was in the city and took his men and went up to Mount Tabor. The Lord discomfited Sisera and his chariots and his host so that he jumped down off his chariot and fled on foot. Barak pursued the chariots and Sisera's army and destroyed them. Sisera fled on foot to the tent of Jael, the woman the Lord used to destroy him. Deborah, Barak, and Jael were willing to be used by God, thereby bringing peace of mind back to the Israelites.

It seemed I was crying to the Lord constantly, but the Lord hears every time we cry, and he is able to deliver us. The Lord can make it difficult for the enemy and cause him to run into the hands of his destroyer. All I had to do was be obedient to what he was telling me to do and control what I allowed to come into my mind.

The people of Israel had felt the mighty oppression of the enemy. They knew that they could no longer settle for second best in their lives; they had to have the best for their children. They had to commit to God their hearts, minds, and spirits. They knew that when the Lord moved, the earth trembled and the mountains melted. I was being oppressed by the spirit of fear. I was allowing it to dictate to my mind how I should act and react. I was settling for second best. My choice could only be the best—the God of all power. My mind had to make its boast in the Lord God almighty, because there is none like him.

I knew I loved the Lord. Judges 5:31 says, "So let all thine enemies perish, O Lord; but, let them that love him be as the sun when he goeth forth in his might. And the land had rest forty years." The translation for *sun* in *Strong's Concordance* is brilliant or shining brightly. I wanted to shine brightly as the Lord did his mighty works in my life.

KEEP THE WEAPON
FROM THE ENEMY

A weapon is an instrument of war.

Second Corinthians 10:3 states, "For though we walk in the flesh, we do not war after the flesh."

Second Corinthians 10:4 states, "For the weapons of our warfare are not carnal, but mighty through God to the pulling down of strongholds."

Second Corinthians 10:5 states, "Casting down imaginations and every high thing that exalteth itself against the knowledge of God, and bringing into captivity every thought to the obedience of Christ."

I had been looking at the outward appearance of situations. Viewing what is happening outwardly only shows what has occurred. Looking deeper into a situation gives a better understanding of what is causing the problem. Seeing what is really happening helps us to face the issues and identify them clearly. It also helps us to understand that in the spirit realm there is a war going on. It may be there is something God is trying to teach and the adversary is trying to keep us from learning. Or the adversary is trying to harm us and the angels are fighting to protect. Or it may be a test to see if you will use your spiritual weapons to fight. I found that the fight at times would be hard, but I knew the strongholds had to come down.

The word of God is like a two-edged sword and is the mightiest weapon we possess. The word of God cuts to the marrow of the bone. It cuts out negative emotions, fears, and doubts. The word of God is the bread of life. The adversary wants you to starve the spirit man. The more you read the word, the more you learn about God; the more you learn about God, the more power you have against spirits like fear. The shield of faith quenches the fiery darts that the adversary will throw to cause our hearts to fail. It is impossible to please God without faith. We must believe that he is able to do great and wonderful works in our lives, even if we cannot see them. The word of God and faith in God assure us that he is able to turn our situations around. Fear is defeated.

The weapons of praise, joy, the love of Jesus, and the power in his name are important. The Lord dwells in the praises of his people. Battles were won by the shouts of praise unto the Lord. There is victory in praise. The joy of the Lord is strength. When tired, weak, and fighting seem impossible, sing, dance, and shout for joy. The wonderful feeling of knowing Jesus loves us gives us strength to continue the fight. Rejoicing in trouble confuses the enemy. When Jesus died on the cross, his love gave us victory over death, hell, and the grave. The love of Jesus heals the broken in heart and spirit. It heals the sickness and diseases, and it helps to renew faith. Everything comes under subjection in the spirit world when you call on the name of Jesus. Hold onto the weapons God has given, and stand on his promises. Fear has to back off.

Mercy is a weapon against fear. God's mercy (compassion and kindness) keeps us. Fear caused me to tell myself that I was showing a lack of judgment because there was a mistake made and it was my fault, when in reality, it was not true. My self-esteem, which was already low, seemed to drop even more. The more I focused on my lack of judgement the higher my anxiety level became, and in my mind, I heard, "God is going to punish you." Fear had showed its ugly head. I had to get control of myself and say, "God is not a tyrant." God is not unkind and ready to pour out his wrath upon me. Jeremiah 31:3 says, "The Lord hath appeared of old unto me saying, yea, I have loved thee with an everlasting love: therefore with lovingkindness have I drawn thee." Psalm 31:7 says, "I will be glad and rejoice in thy mercy: for thou hast considered my trouble; thou hast known my soul in adversities." Psalm 31:8 says, "And hast not shut me up into the hand of the enemy: thou hast set my feet in a large room." God will have mercy on whomever he will, and I was going to glorify him for his mercy, rejoice, and be glad. I had to remember that God's love is an everlasting love. When fear comes, God's mercy says, "I care, and I will help."

My job was to hold on to the weapons God had given me. Holding on to praise, joy, faith, and the word of God—not doubting—will help to be effective in combating fear. A songwriter penned a song that said, "God doesn't want and doesn't need any coward soldiers." I refuse to be afraid of doing the will of God in my life.

BEWARE OF PLAYBACK

In order for me to succeed, I had to hold on to my weapons and not look back on my failures. Paul says in Philippians 3:13, "Brethren, I count not myself to have apprehended; but this one thing I do, forgetting those things which are behind, and reaching forth unto those things which are before." Paul continues to say in Philippians 3:14, "I press toward the mark for the prize of the high calling of God in Christ Jesus." I was going to reach my goal, and I knew I had to press to overcome my fears. I had to forget about those things that were behind. I could not be like Lot's wife and try to take one last glimpse. Playing back the negative experiences in your mind causes fear to take over and destroy the positive experiences that help you go forward. Thinking about what you missed in life—the pains people caused, the shame you experienced, the feelings of regret and doubt—distorts the successes and victories in your life. Avoiding playback helps to press ahead toward the prize. Looking to Jesus helped me to see the great things that are coming now and forever more.

Pressing forward meant I had to embrace and submit to Christ. I felt I was submitting to the Lord, but I was falling short. I desired the word, but I wasn't allowing myself to apply it completely to my life. I had to allow the power of God that was in me to control my actions and reactions. I read in Revelations 20:10 the judgment for the fearful and unbelieving is that they are going to be in the lake that burns with fire and brimstone. The devil is also going to be cast into the lake, along with the beast and the false prophets, and shall be tormented day and night forever. This was a serious reality. It shook me. I wasn't about to let fear take me to this horrible place. I had to run into the arms of the Lord, submitting myself completely to him, yielding to his actions and plan.

Fear had been tormenting me day and night. I would go to bed at night, and not long after falling asleep, I would wake up fearful. I would be thinking about my children, thinking about what had happened the day before that could cause a problem for the day, and thinking about every negative thing that my mind would bring up.

Realizing that my sleep was being deprived, I began to research sleep aids. When I would see articles on how to relax after a busy day, I would read them to get a solution to my insomnia. I heard about using music, listening to nature sounds, and lying still in one position and concentrating on lying still, concentrating on your toes, ankles, legs, etc. until you have reached the top of your head. At that point, you should be asleep. I tried them all. What worked for me was when I began with my toes and prayed for them, thanked God for them, and before I would reach my thigh, I would be asleep. I would awake in the morning rejoicing and thanking God.

What was happening was a light affliction, and as Paul told Timothy in 2 Timothy 4:5, endure afflictions. We must endure afflictions. Continuing to work through these feelings, yielding to the actions and plan of God, was necessary to overcome fear. Christ died and rose again to give us an abundant life. There was nothing I couldn't do with Christ in my life. Paul states in Philippians 2:13, "For it is God which worketh in you both to will and to do of his good pleasure." Everything that was happening in my life was for my good, and he was going to get the glory.

My mind had to change. I had to replace the senseless and unreasonable thinking with my ability to reason and believe God. My mind had to be strong in the knowledge of God. We must not be ignorant of Satan's devices. Changing the mind is difficult because it wants to play back all the things we know, but we must put on the mind of Christ. How would the Lord handle the situation? Getting closer to Jesus in prayer and reading of the word can answer these questions. I had to believe that when I moved, I was moving in the spirit of God, not the spirit of fear.

Romans 12:2 begs the brothers, "And be not conformed to this world, but be transformed by the renewing of your mind, that you may prove what is that good, and acceptable, and perfect will of God."

Second Corinthians 4:16 says, "For what cause we faint not; but though our outward man perish, yet the inward man is renewed day by day."

Colossians 3:10 says, "And have put on the new man, which is renewed in knowledge after the image of him that created him."

God was renewing me with knowledge and understanding. I could not look back.

FROM WHOSE TABLE DO YOU PARTAKE?

First Corinthians 10:21 says, "Ye cannot drink the cup of the Lord, and the cup of devils: ye cannot be partakers of the Lord's table and of the table of devils."

The enemy prepares a table before us to feed to us the things he wants us to digest. He uses whatever he can to feed us his junk food. He uses the media, family members, and other people. The type of food he gives is old wives' tales and fables, human observations, lies, insecurity, doubt, and unbelief. If we allow the enemy to feed us all these different courses, it will bring about a meal that eventually makes us sick. To feast at the table of the Lord, you must cleanse yourself from what the enemy has been feeding you. Repentance starts the cleansing process. Next, get to the root of what is causing you to listen to what the enemy is feeding into your spiritual man. Let God's spirit flow through your spiritual digestive system and clean out all the old fatty tissues that cause the cravings.

Realizing I was listening to what the enemy was saying to me more than what God was saying, I began to fast. Fasting breaks the yokes. I began to think about what fasting really does for the spiritual man.

- The body becomes calm. (Because when you are bound or feeling the pressure of possible bondage, you experience the feeling of nervousness and fear.)
- The mind thinks clearer. (Because when you are in bonds, you can't think outside the bondage box. Everything seems dark and dim.)
- The mind focuses on the things of God. (Because when in bondage, you look back at the negative things and look forward to continual bondage; you can't see yourself free. Jesus gives answers to situations.)
- Fasting slows your reaction process down (slow to anger). (Because when in bonds, you are defensive to what people say or do.)
- You think and do. (You think on what God wants you to do and then strive to do whatever he requires of you.)
- It reveals the hand of the enemy.

- It helps to breaks down oppression, depression, anxiety, and fear.
- It causes you to want to fast more.
- Fasting helps you to see how petty the enemy's devices are compared to the powerful God we serve. There is nothing that the enemy does that is too great for God. There is no bondage or yoke that our God cannot break.
- Fasting humbles you when no one knows you are fasting.
- Fasting causes you to become more devoted to God.

I CAN'T COME DOWN

My God is so great that I knew I had to stand. I had to stay on the wall. The Lord led me to the book of Nehemiah. Nehemiah got permission from the king, after God had put on Nehemiah's heart to rebuild the wall of Jerusalem (Nehemiah 2:11–19). Nehemiah viewed the walls of Jerusalem, which were broken down, and the gates were consumed with fire. He saw the desolation and admonished the people to come with him to build up the wall. Nehemiah began the process of building the wall.

There are times when you find yourself in a distressed situation (grieving, hurting, ill, sad, sorrowful, or troubled) and feel the desolation in your mind. The dry, empty place seems to burn within you. As soon as you decide, "I've got to build myself up and come out of this place," there is always someone who will laugh and say you can't change things.

Sanballant and Tobiah laughed and despised what Nehemiah was about to do. Sometimes the Sanballats and Tobiahs are not people. They are thoughts that come to your mind. Negative forces despise what we are trying to do for ourselves. It may be said that it can't be done, but with Jesus, all things are possible. Let them laugh.

When the people began to build, they rose up and built the sheep gates, set up the door, and sanctified them and the towers. After everything had been sanctified, every man began to build his portion of the wall and repaired it completely.

When we start to rebuild our lives and make the 180-degree turn, consecrate ourselves, purify ourselves from unrighteousness, change our way of thinking, repent, and seek the spirit of God, it's time to work, declaring what God has accomplished in our lives. Fear and doubt will enter the mind to try to hinder the work of God. But greater is he who is in us then he who is in the world.

Nehemiah 4:1 says, "Sanballat was wroth after hearing that they built the wall, and took great indignation, and mocked them." Sanballat and Tobiah conspired for all the people to come together and fight Jerusalem and to hinder the completion of the building. But God's people had a mind to work, and when they heard of the conspiracy, they prayed and set a watch against them day and night. They worked with one hand and held a weapon in the other.

When your spiritual enemy hears of what you are doing to change your life, he becomes wroth, but we must have a mind to work and keep working to build the kingdom. There is always a conspiracy against those who are trying to change their lives for the better.

Nehemiah continued to encourage the people. Nehemiah 4:14 says, "And I looked and rose up, and said unto the nobles, and to the rulers, and to the rest of the people, Be not ye afraid of them: remember the Lord, which is great and terrible, fights for the brethren, your sons, your daughters, your wives, and your houses." There is an assurance that when we seek the Lord, we know that he is going to fight for his people. I had to put on the armor of God, but God would do the fighting.

I had to arm myself and keep building a closer relationship with Christ, to gain more power. Jesus died because he loved us, and he wants to give us an abundant life. He wants us to be victorious, so he gives us the tools for the battle. When I felt anxious and when fear or doubt arose in my mind, I knew if I humbled myself and prayed, I could tell the Lord how I felt and he would give me an answer to help me through those feelings. Jesus tells us we can come unto him, all who are heavy laden, and he will give us rest.

I realized what was happening to me was not about me; it was about what God wanted to do in my life. It was about the soul that needed to know that God is a deliverer. God is in control, even though I felt out of control. I needed to evaluate and determine what was important in my life and then concentrate my energy on those things. Once again, *focus* was the key word. What does God think about what I am doing? Am I pleasing God? Am I allowing God to get the best out of my life? I asked myself these questions.

I realize our lives are tested. I believe we are tested in this life to prepare us for eternal life. The way we handle the test determines the direction we want our lives to go. It is either heaven or hell. God wants us to pass the test. He wants us to be victorious, so he prepares a way of escape with every test. He gives us the book with the answers.

Focusing on my purpose gave new meaning to my life. It was not about what I wanted but what God wanted to do through me. Fear and doubt were trying to hinder me from going forward. Even though the test was challenging, it became easier as I focused on "It's not about me." God is in control of my life, and he knows the direction I want to take. Heaven is my destination. This is only a temporary stop. I had to be about the Father's business.

DISTORTED VISION

Proverbs 3:5 says, "Trust in the Lord with all thine heart; and lean not unto thine own understanding."

Situations take place, and you are unsure of what you should do. You want to be pleasing in the sight of the Lord, but you can't seem to get direction. When our vision is cloudy and we get into an obscure state where we can't think of anything but the situation, the word of God must be our guide.

The verse of scripture says to "trust." David wants us to be confident that God is reliable and will never fail. I believe the Lord wants us to walk safely in him, not relying upon ourselves to figure out the solution to the situations. If I allow the Lord, he will make my vision clear. When you call on the name of the Lord Jesus, he enlightens us. He brings light to the darkness. He puts us on the right path and makes the way clearer. I didn't understand why I was experiencing these tormenting spirits, but I knew if I acknowledge Jesus as my help, he would lead me out of this devastating place.

I asked myself, "Are you a mighty one?"

In the book of Isaiah, chapter 13 talks about God threatening to destroy Babylon by the Medes. Isaiah 13:2 says, "Lift ye up a banner on the high mountain, exalt the voice unto them; shake the hand, that they may go into the gates of the nobles."

Isaiah 13:3 says, "I have commanded my sanctified ones, I have also called my mighty ones for mine anger, even them that rejoice in my highness."

I felt that God wanted to use me as an instrument to destroy the work of the adversary. I had to realize that I was going to conquer this spirit of fear, have a cry of victory, and exalt the name of Jesus. I had been called to be sanctified (set apart) and to be a mighty warrior for the Lord. The word says the mighty were called for his anger. The antics of the enemy anger God. I had to be that mighty one God had called. The mighty are like cannons against the enemy. When we rejoice and exalt the name of Jesus, it is like shooting cannon balls at the enemy.

My body had been reacting to the situations that brought about the feelings of fear. The nervous feeling in my stomach, the battle within my mind trying to figure out what was done wrong, the increased blood pressure, and the restless nights were beginning to take a toll on me. My body is a living sacrifice unto God, and I was allowing fear to break it down. I had to find something to do to counteract what was happening in my body.

Proverbs 15:33 says, "The fear of the Lord is the instruction of wisdom; and before honor is humility." I began to pray and ask God to give me instruction. God gave me instructions. I began to exercise to relieve the stress. I worked with my hands to provide things for my family and others; I crocheted, took piano lessons, and worked at the church. I was presenting my body to Christ. God was also teaching me how to become a Proverbs 31 virtuous woman in the midst of my situation. I could see that this experience was working to make me a better person in more than one way. I had to regain the strength in my body along with strengthening my mind. I could not be mighty reacting to the feelings of fear.

Mighty meant I had to be strong, but at times, I felt my strength was almost gone. I knew the joy of the Lord was my strength. But I had found it difficult sometimes to praise God. I found myself crying unto the Lord but not praising him. The adversary wants us to respond to the flesh. He knows that the flesh wants to feel assured that everything is all right. But when you are in the middle of the situation, it is hard to feel assured everything is okay. Our flesh responds to its senses, including what it sees, touches, hears, tastes, and smells. When we are in a situation, the flesh reacts to what it's sensing and how it feels emotionally. This is how the enemy gains his control. He allows you to hear or see something that causes your emotions to react. Praise and worship are essential to regaining your strength. Praising God gets his attention. His word says if you don't have joy, leap for it. That is an indication that praise is a way to get joy. When we praise God and thank him for everything we are going through, we are becoming mighty in Christ. I begin to praise God in spite of my feelings.

WHAT ARE YOU MEDITATING ON?

Let the words of my mouth, and the meditation of my heart, be acceptable in thy sight, O Lord, my strength, and my redeemer.

—Psalm 19:14

Meditation is focused thinking. It is a skill you learn. Meditation is the opposite of worry. Worry is when you think about a problem over and over in your mind. I began to ask myself, "What am I thinking about during the day? Are my thoughts acceptable in the sight of God? When the Lord looks on my heart, what does he see? Am I pondering over my life and getting no answers? Am I trying to work out problems that can only be handled by the master? Am I allowing the enemy to cause me to meditate on him?" What are you meditating on?

The psalmist David's words came to me, and I began to look at his life. David was consistently thinking on the Lord. He knew what God could do, and he thought about it day and night. He rejoiced in what God could do, had done, and was doing. He had put his trust in the Lord. He admonished the people to love the Lord and to be of good courage. The Lord will strengthen our hearts.

When you love someone, you think about him or her all day. You think about him or her before you go to sleep and wake up with him or her on your mind. You are meditating on him or her day and night. I knew this was what I had to do to love the Lord Jesus Christ.

When you meditate on someone you love, you are happy, content, excited, anticipating being with that person and you feel love in your heart all day. How much more should we give our hearts to Jesus? He died so that we might have an abundant life here on earth and eternal life with him in the place he has prepared for us. We should be excited knowing that he is coming back to take us to that place where he is. The thought came to my mind that when his spirit is in us, love lives in us. If I allow the Lord to have his perfect work in my life, fear must go. I began to meditate on the love of Jesus.

I had to overcome this battle in my mind. Ironically,

one day during a mind battle, I decided to use the tool I had learned, replacing the negative thoughts with the positive. I went into action. I took the negative thought and changed it into a better worst-case scenario. How funny that was to me—changing a negative into a better negative. Fear had not been defeated; it was just looked at in a different light. I realized that I had to practice more, but I rejoiced in the fact that I understood more. I was becoming wiser. In the past, I would not have recognized what was happening. Victory was on the way.

GET UP FROM UNDER THE JUNIPER TREE

The enemy threatens, the pressure is overwhelming, and it feels as though you could die. You want the journey to end. Elijah felt the pressure of fear in 1 Kings 10:4. "But he himself went a day's journey into the wilderness, and came and sat down under a juniper tree: and he requested for himself that he might die; and said it is enough, now, oh Lord, take away my life, for I am not better than my father." Elijah had shown the power of God through the miraculous works he had done, but he allowed fear to cause him to become weakened. He expressed he felt he was no better than his fathers. He lay down under the tree and went to sleep. The Lord sent an angel who prepared for him a meal, awakened him, told him to eat and drink, but Elijah went back to sleep. The angel again awakened him and said, "Eat and drink because the journey is long." Elijah ate and drank and went in the strength of the meal to Mount Horeb. God strengthens us and helps us to go through places in our lives that cause us to want to give up.

Elijah was a mighty man of God, but during a moment of weakness, he didn't know what to do. Relying on the strength of God is our help. When we are weak, he is strong. God had to reassure Elijah that he was not alone. There were those who had not bowed their knees to Baal. There are true men and women of God who will pray for us during our time of distress and anxiety. I had to realize that people were praying for me. God let me know I had to get up from under the Juniper tree. God had shown his mighty acts in my life. I had to get up and go do what I had been appointed to do without doubting.

THIS SICKNESS IS NOT UNTO DEATH BUT FOR THE GLORY (PRAISE) OF GOD

The Lord allows things to come upon us, but they are not to destroy us. The story of the death of Lazarus in the book of St. John, chapter 11, is the perfect example of how God will delay the answer to our request, to get his glory out of our lives. Lazarus's sister sent a message to Jesus to let him know their brother was sick. The Lord waited two days before he left the place where he was. During that time, Lazarus died.

When Jesus arrived and Martha heard, she told Jesus, "Lord, if you had been here my brother would not have died" (John 11:21). "But I know that even now, whatsoever thou will ask of God, God will give it thee" (John 11:22). Jesus assures her that Lazarus will rise again. Martha didn't understand. Jesus said unto her, "I am the resurrection and the life: he that believeth in me, though he were dead, yet shall he live" (John 11:25). "Whosoever liveth and believeth in me shall never die." (John 11:26). Jesus was telling her to believe and she would see the divine intervention of God.

Sometimes we feel that the Lord could have prevented our situation, but we must realize that there is a reason for him allowing the circumstances. Many times we are confused; we look for direction and ask questions. God wants to show his power in our situations.

Fear can become all-consuming, challenging us to the point that we feel defeated, but we have to know that God won't put on us more than we can bear and that he wants the glory out of our lives. Knowing this, we are assured that there is an escape plan.

My mind, when I was fearful, became distracted. It would start to stray and draw me into a conflicting direction. I was struggling to stay focused on the Bible and the correct way to handle the situation. "What if?" would start to lead me away from "No matter what, God is in control."

The scripture in Isaiah 26:3 says, "Thou will keep him in perfect peace, whose mind is stayed on thee: because he trusted in thee."

I came to the realization that change came when I

made an everyday conscientious effort. I woke every day saying, "This is the day the Lord has made, and I will rejoice in it, even if it is difficult, because God is in control." I began to ask God to direct the course I took, including my conduct and my thoughts. I knew his voice and listened to his directions. Listening to God's directions would keep me from listening to other voices that wanted to confuse my mind.

In John 14:27, Jesus says, "Peace I leave with you, my peace I give unto you: not as the world giveth, give I unto you. Let not your heart be troubled, neither let it be afraid."

In John 16:33, Jesus says, "These things I have spoken unto you, that in me ye might have peace. In the world ye shall have tribulation: but be of good cheer; I have overcome the world."

With peace in my life, fear has to find another vessel to encamp about. The mental battles that were going on in my mind were subsiding. Peace is a fruit of the spirit, and I had to learn how to apply it to my life. Peace is something God has given to us to use to overcome the things that take place in this world. The feeling of serenity when fear would arise gave me a feeling of harmony with God. Fear and peace cannot cohabitate.

Now I realized that I had been missing more than just love but also peace. I felt like I did after having my first child: exhausted but overwhelmed with joy and excitement. I tried to explain what had happened to me, but I couldn't put it into words. Until I remembered the verse of scripture in Philippians 4:7 that says, "And the peace of God, which passeth all understanding, shall keep your hearts and minds through Christ Jesus." There was a peace that had come into my life that had surpassed all understanding.

When fear would enter my mind, I would calmly say, to whatever the situation, "God is directing me, so this must be the path I must take." I would declare that my God was a just God and I trusted his decisions. There is nothing this enemy can do to me without the Lord's permission. As long as I live in this world, the spirit of fear will be inevitable; our world is full of fear. But Jesus said that he has overcome the world through his death, burial, and resurrection. Jesus brought salvation to us, and like salvation, peace is not an emotion. It is freedom.

Peace was the answer to my fear, but why did the Lord say I didn't love him? I questioned the Lord. He gave me the answer. Many people say they love God, but when troubles come, they lean to what they know and feel comfortable doing. But it is not always the will of God for their lives.

Trusting in God just doesn't seem to be the answer for many people. They say, "I know this will work,"

"I asked my friend and he [she] gave me the answer," "Society says ..." "Statistics say ..." and many other knowledgeable answers. God wanted me to know that trusting him showed I loved him. But he also wanted me to be loving toward him. What does *loving* mean? Loving means "feeling love; devoted, expressing love." I also looked up the word *devote*. It means "to set apart for a special use or service, to give up (oneself or time, or energy, to some purpose, or person)." I hadn't given up myself to God completely. Giving up means not taking ourselves (our will) back. It has to be "not my will, but thy (God's) will be done." The word *will* means "strong and fixed purpose." My new found freedom and trust in God had put new purpose in my life.

THERE IS A FEAR IN GOD'S PURPOSE/WILL

God's purpose for my life sounded to me like my fears would end, but unlike what I thought, I realized that God's purpose was unknown to me. Now the unknown seemed scary. God has the end in view: purpose. I believe our lives are preordained, not an accident. Romans 8:28 says, "And we know that all things work together to them that love God, to them who are called according to his purpose." He knows the number of hairs on our head, and he tells us not to fear because we are valuable to him (Matthew 10:30–31). He knows what we are thinking before we speak. He knows the beginning and the end. I could only see what was happening now and had heard what the end was going to be, but what about the things that are to come before the end?

When I first became a Christian, I heard about

praying the perfect will of God for my life. I didn't want to pray the perfect will of God for my life because it might not be what I wanted. I struggled with giving God my will. I had been my own problem solver. It was difficult to give it all over to Jesus. I wanted it my way.

Now it was up to me to do it God's way. It was easy giving things to God when I had messed them up. I would pray that familiar prayer. "Lord, if you get me out of this, I will not do it again." But when I thought I was in control, I went about with *my* daily plans. I had to commit totally to the Lord. I had to ask the Lord to influence my thinking, give me instructions for whatever I had to do, organize my day, and be personal with me. Like Moses said, "Show yourself." I wanted Jesus to be strong in my life. I wanted his divine direction.

God helps us to be secure, free from fear, in his purpose for our lives. The book of Joshua is a great example of how to be "successful in the battle of life." (*Thompson Chain-Reference Bible*) It tells how God encouraged and enabled him to win the wars he had to go through to fulfill the purpose of God. Sometimes God would tell him to wait. *He* always let him know he was with him and would never leave him or fail him. Numerous times he would tell him to be strong, to be courageous, and to not be afraid or dismayed.

God also told him to meditate on the law day and night. He wanted him to be obedient to what it said, and if he did that, he would be prosperous and have good success.

I believe God knows his purpose for our lives can be fearful. I believe this because of how often he told Joshua not to be afraid. He reassured his presence was with him in every battle. God knew Joshua had a conquest that required his encouragement for success and God magnified Joshua's victories. Even Jesus had to relinquish his will and fears and say, "Not my will but thy will be done" so that we might have victory in our lives. I realized that this war is forever, but the battle is the Lord's. I wanted to be infinite in my pursuit, being victorious so much so that I frustrated the enemy.

God told Joshua he would give him the victory over the fortified city of the enemy. He told him and his army to march around the wall of the city seven times. After marching around the wall the seventh time, a mighty move of the Earth caused the wall to collapse. What appeared in the natural to be impossible was made possible by the power of God. In his obedience to what God told him, he frustrated the enemy and won the battle. I know there is a divine direction for all our lives.

I believe God gave me a direction that took me

out of my comfort zone. I began to question myself. How was I going to accomplish something that I was unfamiliar doing? I felt intimidated. *Intimidated.* What did that word really mean? It means "to make afraid." I realized that fear was trying to show its ugly head. I had to take control of my thoughts and realize just as God had told Joshua, "Fear not and be of good courage God is with thee." God was with me. I believe God had taken me out of my comfort zone so I could see if I really trusted him and if I was going to allow his will to be done in my life.

WALK IN

Purpose and will—how do you know what they are for your life? I pondered this. How do I know that this is the thing God wants me to do? I began to look back on my life to see how the things I allowed God to control in my life worked. What happened to give me the wonderful opportunities I had received in life? My answer was to pursue, wait until the door opens, and walk in.

I had been pursuing a career after I got out of school, but I wasn't sure what I wanted to do. I tried different occupations and went to school to achieve a career in each field. But I found that they weren't what I wanted. After many years and four children, I found what I really had a desire to become: a teacher.

One day while unemployed, I was working at the church and received a call. I answered the phone, and the individual said there was a desperate need for a preschool teacher. I fit the requirements, applied, and got the job. I enjoyed what I did immensely, but over a short period of time, there was a shift in the administration and the school closed. I was without a job. I remember crying because I loved what I was doing. That day was when I decided to go back to school and become a teacher. Through many struggles, I eventually graduated with my bachelor of arts degree and finished my student teacher training with a letter of high recommendation.

Next was the test. I had to pass a three-part test before I could become an elementary school teacher. I was nervous, but I had completed school on the president's list and had other high levels of achievements. I felt this shouldn't be hard. But to my surprise, I didn't pass. I began to research for help aids and found a class I could enroll in to help me pass the test. I took the class and passed it at the same level of achievement as the original test required. I attempted the test once more and prayed. I asked God to help me pass. Again I didn't pass, missing only by several points. I became frustrated and decided that this wasn't the will of the Lord for me.

I was talking to an individual about my education and my unsuccessful test experience. She told me that I had the qualification to teach young children and suggested that I apply for a substitute teacher position with the Head Start program. I took her advice and was hired. One day while I was working, the social worker from the department came to work with the staff. He began to observe me as I interacted with the children. After I ended my circle, he approached me and asked if I wanted a permanent position. Of course I said yes, and he gave me the number to call. I remember thinking, *I don't really want to work in a preschool setting. I want to be a kindergarten or first grade teacher.* I called anyway, and after hearing the pay and benefits and having the same time schedule as regular school, I had her set me up for an interview.

I practiced for the interview and prayed again. "God, if this is the will for my life, help me to get this job." After completing the interview, I was told to report to the office to begin working. I walked in, and the greatest opportunity of my life began. It lasted until I retired nineteen years later.

We have ambitions and we work to achieve them, but they may only be the preparation for what God has for us. God has greater and more rewarding plans for each of us.

In Revelations 3, John speaks about the Christ that opens and no man shuts and shuts what not man can open. He tells the church that he has opened a door that no man can shut. I believe that every door of opportunity that opens is a door opened by God.

The apostle Paul writes in 1 Corinthians 16:9 that a great door had been opened to him and there were many adversaries. Many times, walking through the doors of opportunity or even walking toward advancing in our everyday lives has its challenges. Fear had been the main adversary in my life trying to keep me from walking through the door the Lord had opened for me.

When the door has been opened, we must boldly walk through. God has given us access, and by our faith in him, we can with assurance achieve what has been offered to us. God wants us to achieve complete victory, reaching the highest possible goal of accomplishment allowed without fear of the what-ifs.

I had to continue walking in the direction the Lord wanted until he shut the door. I had to work at my highest level until completion and continue to let Jesus lead me. I had to stay focused and not allow anything to cause me to sleep and miss out on the wonderful things in store for me.

I am glad that my eyes have been opened to the peace that Jesus has given me. When the doors open and I step inside, I know Jesus is there to calm all my fears and give me the peace that only he can give.

I have to continue to be sensitive to the spirit of the Lord and draw near unto him. I must always remember that he speaks in ways that are miraculous in the eyes of men, by his never changing word, and the soft still voice that can be heard in prayer and meditation. When fear raises its head, I listen for the small sweet voice that says, "Be not afraid."

ARE YOU SURE?

As I continued working my way through this journey, I started to wonder, *Am I really delivered?* I started to observe my reaction and action to the things the adversary of my mind would say to me.

One day I was watching the news, and as I listened, my mind began to play those old tapes. "That could be one of your children." "This is what's going to happen to your child." Recognizing the voice, I began to tell myself to *stop* listening to the adversary, to listen to what is being said, and to not interject my thoughts into the situation. I had to say no before these thoughts overwhelmed my mind.

I noticed my sleep was much better. When I would awake during the early morning and my mind started to wonder with the thoughts of the day, I began to focus on relaxing my body and mind in order to fall back into a deep sleep. I refused to allow my mind to think on anything other than going back to sleep. Shortly I would be asleep again. I would awake feeling mentally and physically strong.

During the times my judgment was incorrect and I messed up, I refused to cry! I took responsibility for my actions. Taking responsibility for my actions and not condemning myself helped me to easily move forward. Refusing to see the consequences as disastrous with no hope, I viewed the situation as an opportunity for God to show he is strong. I believe God wants us to learn from our mistakes. Wisdom and understanding are important attributes to have as we go through our lives.

One day one of my children had a monetary need. He didn't tell me why he needed the money. As I prepared to go and get the money, I thought, *This is the first of the month*. My mind began to try to figure what was wrong. *They must need food, maybe a bill is behind—there must be something wrong.* After a few minutes of trying to figure out what was wrong, I began to say, "Stop! There is nothing wrong." I changed this negative thought to *He does not need anything. He wants to do something that will take extra money.* I took him the money, and as we began talking, he told me that his friends had planned a trip to the snow and he was going. I was excited to know that I had replaced the negative view into a positive outlook, not fearing the outcome.

There were also occasions when the adversary would tell me that I was responsible for something that I had no control over. "If this happens, it is because of what you said or what you did." I had to retaliate and let the adversary know I have no control over what anyone does. I can only be responsible for my own choices.

HOLY BOLDNESS

I spent my whole life saying, "It must be my fault." I remember my teenage years. My friends would go out of town, fifty miles away, to parties on the weekends. My mom would only let me go on occasion. She didn't believe in "partying." I would hear my friends say how much fun the parties were. I would feel resentment toward my mom. But the few times I was able to go the parties, they were not fun. People would be drinking, become angry, and fight. There was a time when we heard a fight breakout and people were pushing and running trying to get out of the five-story building. We saw people who looked as though they had been in a fight and heard that someone had a gun. Each time I would return home safely, I would think I must be the jinx.

When I was a young child, my mother and dad along with my brother and sisters moved to another city. Because of an agreement, I had to stay with my mother's cousin. I believe this was the beginning of the "I am the reason. Why can't I go?" As time passed, I found people would take advantage of me, and I felt it was my fault. People I loved would make demands, and if I didn't comply, they would make me feel guilty. Trying to keep people happy, I complied. I feared that I would hurt them and they would take their love from me and leave me alone. I would coward down.

After finishing school, I left home. I decided that I would not let anyone intimidate me. I put on a façade. I carried myself as being ruthless, standing up to individuals, but fearful of the results of my choices.

I know now that covering up the fear and low self-esteem had to be revealed and destroyed. I could not continue to bluff my way through life. The Lord wanted me to be bold. I refer to it as holy boldness. No longer could I allow people to cause me to put on a fake front or the adversary to tell me, "You are the jinx."

Boldness was necessary to fight in this war. Being bold meant I had to be ready to take risks, face situations head on, and be fearless (Webster's New World Dictionary). Scripture says in Proverbs 28:1, "The wicked flee when no man pursueth; but the righteous are bold as lions." When I first read this scripture, I thought lions were not afraid of any animal, but I asked Google, "What animal does a lion fear?" The response was "The lion is afraid of large mammals like giraffes, hippos, and elephants, but they are also afraid of their day-to-day prey. Every time a hunt takes place, their prey animals are going to try their best to resist." Even though the lion is facing resistance, he shows himself to be bold. I believe God wants us to face our fears and go forward, even if there is resistance.

Isaiah 54:17 says, "No weapon that is formed against thee shall prosper; and every tongue that that shall rise against thee in judgement thou shalt condemn. This is the heritage of the servants of the Lord, and their righteousness is of me, saith the Lord." There is nothing that we face that God will not help us overcome.

I believe Paul is saying in 2 Corinthians 11:20–21 that if men put you in bondage, devour you, try to exalt himself over you, and strike you while thinking you are weak, be bold. I cannot let anyone think they can take advantage of me and abuse me. God has granted that we may come boldly to his throne and have access with confidence by our faith in him.

Even when my fears came to pass, that very thing that I feared would happen did happen. I had to be bold. A heartbreaking event happened that left me fearful. I questioned God. I felt that if he would have interceded, this would not have happened. I felt like

Mary and Martha when their brother Lazarus died. The sisters let Jesus know that if he would have been there, their brother would not have died. They knew Jesus could heal. Christ boldly took authority and told Lazarus to come forth out of the grave.

The adversary told me that God was not pleased and that the situation was not going to get better. I would bring back to my mind that Jesus is the resurrection and the life. All power is in his control. Jesus hung, bled, and died for our sins. The situation looked hopeless, but God still loves his children.

I began to see and hear things that caused me to become afraid and angry with God. This became a very conflicting time. The attack had me in a whirlwind. One moment, I was trusting God, and the next moment, I was confused and asking why. Then one day I heard a soft still voice in my mind say, "Do you love me only for the loaves and fishes?" Jesus was always providing for the people as he taught them. He had taken two loaves of bread and five fish and fed thousands. I had to ask myself, "Do I follow God because of the good things he does, or do I love him because of who he is and his saving power?" I put the what-ifs out of my mind and repented to God. I love the Lord.

The situation did not change and had, what I thought, an awful outcome. But as the initial outcome evolved, I saw something happen. I saw God work. Great things started happening. I saw his hand of protection. I saw him show favor and open doors that no man will shut. I don't know how much more God will do, but I know he is going to have his way. I know his purpose is being accomplished. He is going to perform the work he has started.

First John 4:16 says, "And we have known and believed the love that God hath to us. God is love; and he that dwelleth in love dwelleth in God and God in him."

First John 4:17 says, "Herein is our love made perfect, that we may have boldness in the Day of Judgment: because as he is, so are we in this world."

Boldness was another factor that has helped free me from the fears that were part of my life. Great boldness, as the Bible calls it, comes from our faith in Christ Jesus. It is more than the ordinary. It is the extraordinary. Coming boldly to the throne has helped me to find mercy and grace. Having believed the word of God, I have been able to overcome.

First John 4:18 reinforces that "there is no fear in love; but perfect love casteth out fear: because fear hath torment. He that feareth is not made perfect in love."

I have finally come to an understanding of what God was trying to help me to attain. The Bible says in Proverbs 4:7, "Wisdom is the principal thing; therefore get wisdom: and with all thy getting get understanding." Getting something can take time and energy and a lot of mental power and is sometimes hard. Coming to an understanding of who I am and what was happening to me was a hard mental journey. But I realize I have gained. Getting my fears under control seems so easy now. Taking control of my thoughts along with boldness has freed me from my intimidations.

STRONG CHARACTER

Fear had run me into the arms of God, and he began to change my life. He was building strong character. I learned it takes strong character to face up to fear. *Webster's* definition of character is "the pattern of behavior or personality found in an individual or group; moral constitution, moral strength; self-discipline, fortitude, etc." All of these attributes were increasing in my life. Character is also a "combination of qualities; such as honesty, courage, and integrity that makes a person different than others." The Lord was setting me apart for his use.

The one word that caught my attention in the definition of character was *integrity*. It means to be complete, unbroken, whole, unimpaired, sound, and having sound moral principle. Fear was trying to keep me from being complete in Christ, trying to weaken me physically and spiritually, along with trying to make me think I was incorrect in my actions and judgments.

Fear tried to keep me broken inside. The adversary knows that if he can take my integrity, my quality of life would change and he would be in charge. I am assured if I continue to allow Christ to be in charge, I will have a life that is complete with everything I need and desire. Holding on to my integrity helps me to hold on to a more abundant life.

Proverbs 11:3 talks about integrity. It says, "The integrity of the upright will guide them: but the perverseness of transgressors shall destroy them." As I walk in faith and not fear with the characteristics of Christ I will walk in power. I will have the power to do great things. Proverbs 19:1 says, "Better is the poor that walketh in his integrity than he that is perverse in his lips and is a fool." Fear wanted me not to use good judgment. I continued to read in Proverbs 20:7, and it said, "The just man walketh in his integrity: his children are blessed after him." My overcoming this battle was not just for me but for my children, my grandchildren, and the generations to come.

God didn't only want to build my character, but he wanted my character to be strong. I explored the definition of the word *strong*. It addressed "performing well or in a normal manner, not being easily affected or upset; morally powerful; having strength of character, having special competence (power) or ability, leading with firm authority, powerfully made, built tough, hard to capture, able to resist and endure attack, not easily defeated, deep rooted, powerful in wealth, having a powerful effect, zealous." I believe God wanted me to develop these characteristics to become a powerful witness for his glory.

No longer could I be upset with what was happening to me. The struggles that were taking place were coming to make me strong by testing my endurance and my faith. The apostle Paul urged Timothy to endure afflictions as a good soldier of Christ Jesus. He also told him not to get entangled with the things of this life now that he had become a soldier of Christ. Looking at what is happening in the world can bring on the spirit of fear. We cannot be like the ostrich when he senses danger and cannot run away and then flop to the ground and remain still, with its head and neck flat on the ground in front of it, blending in with the color of the soil. We must not become confused. These ups and downs in life are part of God's plan.

My emotions were now, more than ever before, being captured by the power and authority of Jesus that was invested in me through faith. I had to stay stern in my belief and purpose. Now I laugh instead of cry. Now positive emotional reactions are overriding those exhibited in fear. Anxiety was overtaken by peace, sadness by joy, and anger with understanding; low self-esteem was overtaken by affirmation and confidence; fear was overtaken by determination, meditation, faith, love, and trust.

There is no more closing my eyes and screaming. I have the ability to stand up, look the situation in the eye, and allow the power of God to take over, never forgetting I was not doing it on my own. Fear will always raise its ugly head, but there will be no more ignoring its presence. I will resist it with the strength God is giving me. In the book of James, he admonishes us to resist the devil and he shall flee. When you resist, you fight against the actions that are coming against you. I was a fighter when I was young, so now I have to fight the adversary of my soul with all the power invested within me. I have to open my eyes and shout the cry of victory.

Those deep-rooted things that were in my life that were producing fear have been replaced with the rooting and grounding of *love*.

Ephesians 3:17 says, "That Christ may dwell in your hearts by faith; that ye, being rooted and grounded in love."

Colossians 2:7 says it this way: "Rooted and built up in him, and stablished in the faith, as you have been taught, abounding therein with thanksgiving."

As God began to strengthen my character, the old, weak character tried to reappear. One day I was excited about what God was doing. I began to express my excitement and an individual tried to extinguish the excitement. The weak character wanted to cry, but the strong character subdued that urge, and standing strong, I began to understand what was happening. The excitement of an individual is not always enjoyed by others. I held on to the joy and excitement that can only come from a delivering God.

I began to look back on my life. I realized the labels and the words that myself and others had spoken into my life were words that provided the ground for the spirit of fear to grow. I always used the word *shy* to describe myself. The word means "easily frightened" or "timid." I was told in a negative way that I was "going to be just like your mama," by someone I respected and loved. I was told by someone I loved that they could be happier with someone else. There were many times I wanted to run away, which is one of the main attributes of fear. The words of rejection and the other things I discovered in my life harvested fear.

Knowing who you are and why you are alive helps build strong character. Jesus knew why he was on earth and what he had to suffer. He stayed strong when he healed ten men and only one came back to say thank-you. He showed his strength and power when he told the one who came back that he was making him complete physically and spiritually. As the crowed declared crucify him, before he hung his head and died, he said, "Father, forgive them." What an amazingly strong character.

I believe that God wanted to build that same type of character in me. Jesus is our prime example. He wanted me to bless and not cure, to forgive those who hurt, and to crush fear in my life now and forever.

As I continue to walk in this transforming process, I am aware that change happens as a result of passion and commitment. I had to continue to let God work in my life. The strong love and affection I have for the Lord and the emotional drive to be better will help me to advance and go through doors I cannot imagine. I have committed my life to God, and he has made me a promise that when I come to him, he will not reject me. He will supply all my needs according to his riches. I had to continue to get even closer to God, now more than before.

COME UP FROM THE BOTTOM

O ne day a friend of my husband asked him if he wanted some goldfish. He had an abundance of them in his outdoor pond. My husband called me and asked if I wanted them, and I said yes.

I brought three of the fish home. After putting them into the tank, I noticed they were swimming frantically, bumping into the sides of the tank, and swimming close to the bottom. I already had a smaller goldfish in the same tank. It was familiar with me. It would come to the top of the tank to get food. If I placed my finger to the tank and move it upward, my fish would follow my finger. She would come to the top and feed. But these fish would run and gather into a huddle in a corner of the tank when I would move toward the tank. I knew they were afraid.

I noticed one day that the new fish had caused my

fish to swim into a corner and they had her blocked, making it difficult for her to swim out. I watched them for several days and thought, *Are they going to kill her?* As I observed days later, they stopped cornering her and started following her around in the tank, seemingly thinking she was a friend and not an enemy.

During feeding time, I would go over to the tank and motion for my smaller fish to come to the top, and as usual, she did, but the other fish stayed at the bottom until the fish food floated to the bottom. After days of feeding them, I noticed that one of the other fish noticed the smaller fish was going to the top and tried to swim to the top. It quickly swam up, grabbed the food, and then went back down to the bottom. The other fish continued to feed at the bottom. I thought, *Could they possibly be afraid to try?*

I decided to separate the smaller fish from the others. She was a calm fish who sometimes would rest on her back. But with the other fish chasing her and swimming close to her, she seemed to not be able to rest. They would actively swim back and forth.

After separating the smaller fish, the other fish once again stopped swimming and began to huddle in the corners. I would turn the light on, and they would move frantically around the tank. It seemed that they were also afraid of the light.

It puzzled me. *Why aren't the fish going to the top*

to get food? My fish would wait at the top in the area where I fed her, to be fed. That would be my indicator that I had not fed her. The other fish, except for one, continued to swim at the bottom. But the one who had ventured to the top and found food there tried again. I was telling my sister about my fish, because she also had the same kind of fish. She began to tell me that I needed to add a chemical to the water to take out the ammonia. She said her fish would stay at the bottom if the ammonia content was high. She gave me something to use, and I brought it home and added it to the water.

A week passed, and the same two fish continued to feed at the bottom.

The fish that had started to make several trips to the top began to go to the top when he heard the tank opening. I also noticed when the light came on the other fish would continue to hide, but the fish that was different—same species but different—began to swim around even when the light came on seemly unafraid. I believed this fish realized that there was fresh food that he didn't have to wait for at the top and that the light was not to be feared.

I wondered if the other fish would change. Finally one morning about a month later, I fed my fish, and every one of them swam to the top. I was curious to see if there had been a change in their reaction to the light. I noticed that when the light came on, they seemed startled, but in a few seconds, they swam in the direction of the light. I was pleased that they all chose not to be completely satisfied with the food that slowly drifted to the bottom and being content in the dark. I believe God had me observe what was happening in the world of my fish to show me what fear can do to your life if allowed.

I related this scenario to my life. I had been thinking of myself on a level lower than God desired. As I revised my life once more, I remembered how my friends would tease me, laugh at me, and bully me into fighting. They never realized that every time they would do these things, my self-esteem would decline.

I was being raised by my cousins who had raised my mother. She had an adult son, but she had wanted a daughter and I had become that daughter at the age of three months. They provided for me comfortable shelter and good food. My mom dressed me in delightful clothing and provided the best toys. I couldn't have everything I wanted, but everything I had was satisfying. Even though everything was high quality, I felt unloved.

Somewhere in my mind, I found myself believing that I was the underdog. As a young child, I searched to find a friend, someone who would let me be me. I went from one friend to another. I struggled to answer the question "What am I doing wrong?" I would hear in my mind, "You aren't good enough." I remember my mom telling me I should be like my friend. Maybe I needed to be like someone else. Maybe I was not good enough.

As I grew into a teenager, I pushed to be the best socially but was at the bottom in my mind. I was that young teen who just couldn't seem to do it right. I remember falling in "love." My friends and I went swimming with this young man and his friends. I really liked him, and I wanted him to like me. I decided to flirt with him. I swam under the water and grabbed his legs. I startled him and he kicked me. He knocked the air out of me, and I came up for air as though I was drowning. Because I was in the four-foot side of the pool, my friends laughed. I was embarrassed and felt the young man couldn't like someone like me.

As well as being socially clumsy, I also felt like an ugly duckling. I was under the impression that I was not as attractive as my friends. My perception was that boys would not like me. I felt I had to be more than what I was. Since I failed with "love," I attempted to be an athlete. I signed up for the track team. During one AAU meet, I had to run the fifty-yard dash. The starter signaled, and in my mind, I heard the word *go*. I began to run, not realizing that the gun had fired for a false start. Someone had faulted and I didn't know. Once again, my friends laughed, and I was embarrassed.

As I grew, I decided I was going to be successful. I worked hard at being the best, even though many times I failed. But I learned to laugh with others as they laughed at me. But inside was a fearful person, in the bottom of the tank.

After finishing high school, I was ready to go out into the world and become successful. I enrolled in a junior college for one year then I decided I needed to leave my mom's house. I moved to Oakland, California, seeking the success I desired. I went from working at a fast food restaurant to becoming a partner in a restaurant business. I thought I was on my way to success. But instead of arriving into the world of success, I arrived into the world of drugs, alcohol, and violence.

Now my fears were physical and real. The business closed, and eventually we moved to Kansas. The drugs increased, and now my love was for a man who was addicted to drugs. We would fight. He would come home after drinking with his friends and the fight would begin. The fear of not knowing what to expect when he came home was there, but I would not let him know. I fought. I refused to let him know I was afraid. One day I felt threatened and was afraid. I had a gun. I went to the top of the stairs and told him I would shoot. Even though I was afraid, I possibly would have shot him, but I heard my child say, "Mama, don't shoot Daddy."

I found myself in a criminal world where guns and police were involved, far away from home. One day, my son and his father had gone out together. When they returned home, my son, who was sitting in the back seat, got out of the car excited and said to me that he and Daddy had gone to the park. I was happy until he told me the rest of the story. There was a man at the park, and he and daddy were fighting. Daddy left, and the man shot at the car. "Look, Mama. See the hole?" My heart dropped. The bullet had passed inches from where my son had been sitting. I was at the bottom of the tank and not knowing how to get to the top.

Because the addiction had started to destroy our home, we looked for change. My husband enrolled in a program for drug addiction. During a counseling session, I was told I was codependent. I didn't understand what it meant then, but now I know. Codependency was the reason I had allowed myself to stay in this lifestyle. Codependency is a term used to describe "belonging to a dysfunctional, one-sided relationship where one person relies on the other for meeting nearly all of their emotional and self-esteem needs" (Psych Central). It had developed from my desire to be loved and the need to love someone, also believing within myself, "I can help and make a change." Unfortunately, change did not come.

One day I realized, whether there was ammonia at the top of the tank or not, I had to get to the top. I didn't know what was going to be at the top, but I knew I had to get there. I devised a plan to get to California, but in my mind, I believed I would go back. I felt things would be better after I went back. I shared my feeling with a woman on the bus. I met her in the ladies room. She initiated the conversation by saying, "I have been watching you and your children; they are well behaved." I thanked her, and before I knew it, I had told her my life story. She looked at me and said, "You are not going back." I never saw her again.

I remember getting off the bus after arriving from Kansas, sitting on my suitcase while holding my three-month-old with my other three children standing close, and thinking I could kiss the ground. I was so glad to be home. When it was time to return to Kansas, I knew I could not go back. I informed my husband I was not coming back. He began to say the things he said throughout our marriage that had caused me to stay. There were times when I wanted to break down and cry, but I resisted, and when he had finished, he said, "I guess you're not coming back." I was at the top.

Soon after I returned to California, I had my encounter with Jesus. The word fed me the bread of life. I slowly began to rise higher and higher. I would wait at the top until I was fed and rest at the bottom until I wanted another feeding. Like my small fish, I would spend a lot of time at the top looking for something from God.

As I ventured to the top, things started to change in my life. I returned to California with nothing but a one-week change of clothes for myself and my four children. After a short period of time, I found a job and rented a three-bedroom house. I was at the top now, and God was now feeding me. He had protected me at the bottom, but now he was feeding me. I moved into the house, and in a corner of the garage, the lady who had lived there before had left expensive clothes. I asked if she wanted them. She said no and told me to throw them away. I began to look at the clothes; they were all my size. There were leather coats and brand-name clothing.

I was able to continue to advance as I rose to the top. I was able to purchase a newly built home in a small community where I raised my children and completed my education.

The life I had lived left scares that I didn't think would affect my life. But I was wrong. I had to let God reshape my life by allowing him to show me how to take control of my emotions. I believe that my recent encounter with fear was to show me that some of the residue of the pass still remained. I know my fears had to be revisited in order for God to introduce me to the new and improved me.

At the top is an expression that connotes success. Many people relate success as bright lights, luxurious homes, expensive cars, and more money than you can spend in a lifetime. Indeed that is success, but for me, it was the accomplishment and the satisfaction of knowing that the "me" who was lost at an early age had been found. I read a quote from the late John Wooden, head coach at the University of California, Los Angeles. He defined *success*. "Success is peace of mind, which is a direct result of self-satisfaction in knowing you made the effort to do your best to become the best that you are capable of becoming." Success is truly peace of mind.

AT THE TOP

I noticed that one of the new fish who had come to the top to feed no longer would swim to the top. It would wait until the food fell to the bottom. I contemplated why it went back to the bottom. I also noticed that the two fish who now fed at the bottom had joined together. They swam close to one another, following the other fish around and bumping into him on occasions. I didn't realize that they had started to bully the fish who ventured daily to the top for his food. I noticed that he started to look different. Some of his fins and scales were missing. He was bruised. I noticed he moved away whenever they would approach him. Eventually he began to stay at the top of the tank. I believe the Lord brought to my mind a familiar story in the Bible after seeing what occurred in the fish tank.

Jacob was a man who had his name changed to Israel after having an encounter with an angel of God. Jacob had twelve sons. One of his sons was named

Joseph. Jacob loved Joseph and made him a coat of many colors. The Bible says that Joseph's brothers were jealous of him and conspired against him. They threw him into a pit and told their father that he was killed by an animal. Unknown to his brother, there were men who found him, and he was eventually taken to Egypt to Potiphar. Potiphar was an officer of Pharaoh. The Lord was with Joseph, and he advanced in Potiphar's house. Unfortunately, Potiphar's wife wanted Joseph. When he refused her, she accused him of trying to lie with her.

Joseph found himself charged and thrown into prison. Once again God was with him and gave him favor with the keeper of the prison. He was placed over the prisoners. God had given Joseph the ability to interpret dreams. Pharaoh had a dream and wanted the interpretation and Joseph was sent to interpret this dream. After Joseph interpreted the dream, he was placed in charge of Pharaoh's house and all the people. He was made great in Egypt. When the famine Joseph had seen in Pharaoh's dream began, Jacob, now named Israel, sent his sons to Egypt to get food.

Joseph hid his identity from his brothers. He made some stressful requests of them and accused them of stealing. After a short period of time, he revealed himself to his brothers and sent for his father. They were all welcomed into the land of Goshen by Pharaoh. They lived prosperously in the land.

Joseph, his brothers, and all that generation died. The children of Israel were multiplying and were mighty men. They formed a large population of Egypt. During this time, a new king rose up in Egypt, and he didn't know Joseph. He was afraid that the people would join with the enemy and fight against them, overtake them, and take the land. He ordered that they be made to work hard and serve. He oppressed them. But God had a plan, and he rose up Moses to deliver the people. God sent plagues upon Egypt to force Pharaoh to release the Israelites. After the death of this son, Pharaoh released the people but later pursued them.

When the children of Israel saw that Pharaoh and his army were encamping by the sea, they became afraid and cried unto the Lord. Moses told the people not to fear, to stand still, and see the salvation of the Lord. He assured them that the Lord would fight for them. Moses extended his rod, and God destroyed Pharaoh's army in the Red Sea. The Israelites had been delivered from the mighty oppression of Pharaoh. They had come up from the bottom to the top.

The Israelites left Egypt prosperous. The Egyptians sent them away with jewels of silver, jewels of gold, and all of the things they needed for their journey. They took their large flocks and herds of cattle. There were over 600,000 men, women, and children.

With all the wealth God had allowed Israel to leave possessing, after they crossed over to the freedom side, they began to mummer and complain, wanting to go back to Egypt.

God's deliverance provides a person everything they need to stay delivered. He delivers with a strong hand. Difficult trails must cause us to press forward, toward what God has in store. It is not time to go back down to the bottom and feed.

Deuteronomy 28:12 states, "The Lord shall open unto thee his good treasure, the heaven to give the rain unto thy land in his season, and to bless all the work of thine hand: and thou shalt lend unto many nations and thou shalt not borrow."

Deuteronomy 28:13 declares, "And the Lord shall make thee the head, and not the tail: and thou shalt be above only, and thou shalt not be beneath; if that thou hearken unto the commandments of the Lord thy God, which I command thee this day, to observe and to do them."

Jesus died so that we might have life more abundantly. He wants us to acknowledge him in everything we do—in every failure and every accomplishment, in good times, and in difficult times. I believe these times make for an abundant life. Paul, in the book of 2 Corinthians, gives a variety of experiences that created his ministry. Some were difficult, and others were pleasurable. In chapter 8:2, he puts it this way about the church of Macedonia: "How that in a great trial of affliction the abundance of their joy and their deep poverty abounded unto the riches of their liberality?"

We must continue to venture forward. The higher we go in Christ, the richer we become, not only in the blessing of God but also the spiritual riches of Christ. Whatever you receive at the top, give God the praise and acknowledge that he helped you to attain the good gifts. He is the giver of good gifts. Remember to give him praise.

MEOW: "HELP ME"

I believe God used nature to teach me spiritual things. I have owned dogs before, but I never wanted to have a cat as a pet. God used a cat to show me his love.

One hot day in July, my sisters and a friend came to join me for lunch at my house. After we had eaten lunch, I began to make homemade ice cream. I needed something that was in the freezer, which was in the garage. The garage had to be entered from outside. I walked outside and saw a small, young cat. The cat looked up at me and with her big eyes said, "Meow." The sound that I heard from the cat was a cry of help. I tried to motion the cat away, but she cried, "Meow." I knew the cat was lost or had ran away from home. She was soft as she passed by my leg. She appeared to have been well cared for and was not frightened of people. I told my guest that I had a cat outside and I hoped that it would leave, but that was not the case.

I went out again, and she was still there in front of the door.

My sisters and their friend came outside and saw the cat. When they came out, the cat moved close to me, lay down next to me, and placed its head on my foot. Phillis said, "Oh, she loves you." Again I said, "I don't want a cat." My youngest sister insisted on me giving the cat water. I knew this was going to be a start of something I didn't want, but it was hot so I gave the cat water then we went back inside. My sister told me she would take the cat's picture and use the neighborhood app to see if someone would respond to her lost cat advertisement. After everyone had left, I remembered I had leftover fish and fed my newfound guest. This cat had touched my heart.

I had to go to Bible study class, and as I was leaving to go out the door, a thought came to my mind. That is the way Jesus drew me. He drew me by his love. Just like the cat had touched my heart when she rested next to me and placed her head on my foot, the Lord showed his love for me and touched my heart.

Jeremiah the prophet says in Jeremiah 31:3 that the Lord appeared to him and said that he loved him with an everlasting love. The Lord told him that he had drawn him with lovingkindness. I believe the same love that the Lord had for Jeremiah he has for me and anyone who will receive his love.

Reflecting back, I was like the little cat. I was living in a confused mental state. I was crying for help, but I couldn't be heard. Unknowing to me, Christ was listening. God put in my path a woman who saw the hurt inside me. She grew close to me and befriended me. I saw the love of Christ radiating in her life.

She showed me how to walk as a Christian. We had children close to the same age. One day we went out to enjoy the day with our children. A&W Root Beer allowed children under the age of five to have a free root beer. We stopped to get the children one. We had boys who were only months apart in age. My son was four, and her son was five. When we ordered, she ordered a regular root beer for her son instead of the free drink that was offered. I commented that her son looked four and added, "Get him a free drink." She nicely explained that she wouldn't do that because it was lying. I had never seen that kind of truthfulness before. I didn't know then, but I know today she was showing me how to walk in truth and love God.

God used her to comfort me. There would be times when my husband would come home after drinking. To hear the voice of my drunken husband caused me to become angry. I would call her to complain. She asked me if he was trying to start a fight. The answer was no. She told me to be kind and show him love. I didn't want to hear the advice that was given. But I followed the instructions. Even through my complex situations, she would calmly talk to me and let me know she was there to help. She would end our conversation with "I love you."

I realized I was in a difficult position. I was allowing myself to be mentally and physically abused. I was taking chances that could have destroyed my life. I was fearful that at any moment there would be a knock at the door and the police would run through the door looking for my husband. Even though my life was complicated, God provided help by sending my friend Jean to encourage me and demonstrate the love of Christ. She allowed me to be who I was and did not require me to be what she thought I should be. She recognized my dilemma and she extended mercy and love, not criticism. Her hope for me was that I might have a better life.

Jeremiah 18:3–4 describes what God was doing in my life. Jeremiah said, "Then I went down to the potter's house, and, behold, he wrought a work on the wheels." "And the vessel that he made of clay was marred in the hand of the potter: so he made it again another vessel, as seemed good to the potter to make it." I had been marred, and God had to make me over again. I am glad that God used Jean to lead me to the potter. She still has a powerful influence in my life. She is still helping me to grow closer to Jesus, the one who has our lives in his hand.

In Jeremiah 18:6, the Lord asks, "O house of Israel, cannot I do with you as this potter? saith the Lord. Behold, as the clay is in the potter's hand, so are ye in mine hand, O house of Israel."

God wants us to be overcomers and be wise, knowing the path of life and accepting its trials. As we go through this life, we will come out as pure gold if we hold on to our faith in Jesus Christ, our Lord, and keep our hands in the potter's hand, allowing him to mold us into what he wants us to be: vessels of honor.

I believe God allowed me to experience fear to show me how much more I needed him in my life and to become an individual who not only experienced fear but has been set free, no longer restrained by its tormenting power. I want to acknowledge him in all my ways. Now that I am at the top, I must be a fisher of men. I must make known to others how God can heal us by his word when we apply it to our lives. He is ready to wipe away the tears that fear may bring from your eyes and keep you from the fear of evil. He wants to establish a covenant with you that will be everlasting. I believe these few, but powerful, words that God has given me will help someone today.

God wants us to be helpers one to another, and as we receive insight, we will be able to help others.

I want to end with this scripture in Psalm 34:4: "I sought the Lord and he heard me, and delivered me from all my fears."

STRATEGIES AGAINST FEAR

R elax your body and mind: (a) Get plenty of sleep; (b) "Think on those things that are true, honest, just, pure, lovely, of a good report, if there be any virtue, if there be any praise think on these things" (Philippians 4:8); (c) Focus on affirming who you are (I am God's child, he loves me, and there is nothing good that he will withhold from me.); (d) Take a deep breath and give the situation to God.

- Give thanks and Gratitude to God. When you give thanks endorphins are released to relax tension and reduce the stress and suffering it can create. (Hills Physicians)
- Faith (I believe it that settles it.)
- Control your thoughts

- Make a list of positive attributes so you can make reference to them.
- Pray (Find a secret hiding place where you can focus on the Lord and hear him speak. Let it be your sweet resting place.)
- Recognize the markers of fear; what if; you are not...., etc.
- Jesus loves you. Stand still, be quiet, and see the salvation of the Lord.
- Do something for God (visit the sick, show love to family, friends and your neighbor, tell someone about the goodness of Jesus)
- Read the promises of God
- Shout, Dance, and Praise God
- Remember to keep the spiritual man fed daily with the word of God.
- Instead of reacting, wait and see the glory of God.
- Hold on to your weapons and fight on!

HOW LOVE
CONQUERS FEAR

First John 4:7 says, "Beloved, let us love one another; for love is of God; and every one that loveth is born of God, and knoweth God."

First John 4:8 says, "He that loveth not knoweth not God; for God is love."

The word is God and God is his word (Saint John 1:1).

- When fear attacks the mind, sound decisions are impaired. God's forgiveness through the shedding of his blood gives us a fresh start. This act of love calms the threat fear imposes.

- When fear announces its *attack on your life, health, job, home, finances,* love proclaims in Second Chronicles 7:14, "If my people, which are called by my name, shall humble themselves, and pray, and seek my face, and turn from their wicked ways; then will I hear from heaven, and will forgive their sin, and will heal their land." Verse 15 says, "Now mine eyes shall be open, and mine ears attent unto the prayer that is made in this place." Saint John 15:7 says, "If ye abide in me, and my words abide in you, ye shall ask what ye will, and it shall be done unto you."

- When fear comes to your mind to violently stir your emotions, love tells us to stir up the gift of God. "God has not given us the spirit of fear, but of power, and of love and of a sound mind."

- When fear causes you to become anxious, love reminds us to; "Be careful [*anxious*] for nothing; but in everything by prayer and supplication with thanksgiving let your request be made known unto God" (Philippians 4:6).

- When fear tries to alarm you and make threats, love says, "Fret not" (Psalm 37:1). There is no weapon formed that will prosper against you (Isaiah 54:17).

- When fear tries to condemn you, love says, "There is therefore now no condemnation to them which are in Christ Jesus, who walk not after the flesh, but after the Spirit" (Romans 8:1).

- When fear says *God doesn't care,* love shows compassion. Hebrews 4:15 says, "For we have not an high priest which cannot be touched with the feeling of our infirmities; but was in all points tempted like as we are, yet without sin." Hebrews 4:16 invites us to come boldly unto the throne of grace that we may obtain mercy, and find grace to help in time of need.

Love defeats fear. Charity which is the love of God for mankind suffers with us in the tormenting times. It shows kindness toward us and is patient when it is difficult for us to understand or obey. Love does not rejoice when the adversary gets the win and it never fails. (First Corinthians 13:4-7).

Fear is a bugaboo: a bugbear, "Anything causing seemingly needless or excessive fear or anxiety." (*Webster's New World Dictionary*)

God is inimitable: "He cannot be imitated or matched; too good to be equaled or copied." (*Webster's New World Dictionary*)

THE AUTHOR'S BIOGRAPHY

Raised in a small town in Northern California, She is married and has four wonderful children. She raised her children as a single mother after her divorce. She is now remarried to a wonderful man who loves God. She is a retired educator of young children and a licensed minister. She received an Associate of Art Degree in Early Childhood Education at Sacramento City College and a Bachelor's Degree in Liberal Studies from Sacramento State University.

She has worked in ministry for 38 years. She has been a licensed minister 15 years. She is a Sunday school teacher and has received a National Sunday School Association Teachers Certificate from the Pentecostal Churches of the Apostolic Faith, Inc., also a certificate of achievement from the National Teachers Training Course and a certificate of excellence from the Christian Education and Leadership Institute.

She loves to laugh and enjoys life. She delights in traveling, especially visiting her family and friends.

When she is home she enjoys crocheting, music, singing, playing the piano and baking. Her husband said, "She will bake a cake any time of the day or night." She enjoys shopping and eating out with her family and friends. Decorating her home is another pleasurable experience. She attends the gym regularly and enjoys aerobics and group strength training classes.

ACKNOWLEDGEMENTS

I want to thank my family and friends who saw my desire to write this book and encouraged me. They helped to push me toward completion and I want to express my appreciation. The journey was difficult, but with people rallying to help me, I have accomplished my dream. This book is to give knowledge to some and hope to others.